TAKING PART IN THE SECOND WORLD WAR

On Land

Ann Kramer

W
FRANKLIN WATTS
LONDON • SYDNEY

IN ASSOCIATION WITH

IMPERIAL WAR
MUSEUM

This edition 2011

First published in 2010 by Franklin Watts

Franklin Watts
338 Euston Road
London NW1 3BH

Franklin Watts Australia
Level 17/207 Kent Street
Sydney, NSW 2000

A CIP catalogue record for this book is available
from the British Library.

Dewey number: 940.5'4'00922

ISBN 978 1 4451 0639 7

Printed in China

Franklin Watts is a division of Hachette Children's Books,
an Hachette UK company.

www.hachette.co.uk

Editor: Sarah Ridley
Design: Billin Design Solutions
Editor in Chief: John C. Miles
Art director: Jonathan Hair

With many thanks to Nick Hewitt and the staff at the Imperial
War Museum's Document, Sound and Photograph Archives.

Picture credits: All images copyright © Imperial War Museum unless otherwise stated.

Front cover: Main pic BU 12271, inset H 37169, background B 5114, H 9234, top right B 12607
Back cover: B 013038, B 010651, NYT 007633D
Insides: page 1 O 000087; 4 NYT 007633; 5 top O 000087, bottom MH 013585; 6 H 002917;
7 top D005149, bottom H 009234; 8 H 014291; 9 top H 026574, middle H 024517, bottom K 005926;
10 top F 004689, bottom H 001619; 11 HU 041240; 12 E 018474; 13 top E018542, bottom E 020242;
14 NA 006813; 15 top NA 015079, bottom NYP 027322; 16 E 018977; 17 F 003744; 18 NA 012275;
19 top NA 008953, bottom B 013038; 20 SE 000134; 21 top IB 000283, bottom SE 000533;
22 B 010651; 23 top NA 000853, bottom H 037859; 24 top E 014919, bottom B 008050;
25 top B 008256, bottom CM 005442; 26 B 005114; 27 top B 010245; bottom BU 003728;
28 top EA 065948, bottom BU 012271; 29 NA 012703

Contents

On land

At 11 o'clock on a Sunday morning, 3 September 1939, British people tuned into their radios to hear the Prime Minister announce that Britain was at war with Nazi Germany. The Second World War had begun. It continued until 1945.

Most people did not want war but under Adolf Hitler, Germany had become a powerful and aggressive military force. In 1938 Germany annexed (took over) Austria and the following year occupied Czechoslovakia. On 1 September 1939, Germany invaded Poland. Britain and France, who had promised to defend Poland, declared war on Germany.

On land

The Second World War started in Europe but spread worldwide. Battles took place in the air, at sea and on land. British soldiers fought in Europe, North Africa and Southeast Asia. They fought in deserts, jungles and on the European mainland. Canadian, Indian, Australian, New Zealand and other Commonwealth troops fought with them and, from 1941, so too did Americans and Russians. Infantry (foot soldiers), artillery (big guns), tank (armoured) forces, engineers and medics all had vital roles.

It's official, 1939

A newspaper placard in London announces what many people hoped would not happen — that war had been declared. The Second World War began on 3 September 1939. Across Britain and throughout the British Empire young people volunteered for military service.

4

> *"I began thinking, 'Is it going to be like the First World War?' when thousands of men were killed... I thought, 'Is it going to be a repeat? What's going to happen to my brothers?'"*
>
> *Evelyn White, civilian, Birmingham*

Changes

During the First World War (1914–18) millions of young soldiers had died, advancing on foot against machine guns. No one wanted this to happen again. In the First World War, the army still used horses and the employment of tanks was a new development.

Off to war

A week after war was declared, British soldiers — members of the British Expeditionary Force (BEF) — had sailed for France. These soldiers are marching through Cherbourg.

The Second World War saw changes. Armies made greater use of tanks and armoured vehicles, which meant they could move faster, manoeuvre and smash through enemy lines. More powerful weapons were developed and radio communications were better. Fighter and bomber aircraft provided support. Even so, casualties were enormous.

Women auxiliaries

Posters appealed for women to join the ATS — the Auxiliary Territorial Service, the women's branch of the army. Women could join at a labour exchange or army recruitment centre.

ASK FOR INFORMATION AT THE NEAREST EMPLOYMENT EXCHANGE OR AT ANY ARMY OR A.T.S. RECRUITING CENTRE

Call up

When war began, 158,000 soldiers were sent to France to defend the French-Belgian border. Recruiting offices had opened and men were encouraged to enlist.

Britain's army in 1939 consisted of about 897,000 men but it needed more. From July 1939 the government introduced conscription. Men between the ages of 18 and 41 could be called up. A few, known as conscientious objectors, refused to fight.

Charge

As part of a training exercise, soldiers of the Black Watch charge over trenches with fixed bayonets. Tactics such as these had been used in the First World War.

Training

Recruits were issued with khaki battledress and sent to army camps for training. Older soldiers knew what war meant — some had served in the First World War — but younger recruits had little idea of what they might face. Feelings varied from excitement to fear and a sense of duty.

Training was intense as experienced soldiers turned younger civilians into fighting men. Recruits learned to drill, polish equipment and how to charge and fight. Basic training lasted six weeks, then recruits were sent to a regiment. Some joined the infantry as foot soldiers. Others went to artillery regiments to use big guns, or to the Royal Tank Regiment or Royal Armoured Corps. After 1940, some joined The Parachute Regiment. Not all men had combat roles: some joined the army as medics, signallers, engineers or cooks.

Commonwealth soldiers

By 1945 more than 3.5 million had served in the British Army. Some recruits came from all over the British Empire. They included Indians, Canadians and Australians. Here, Muslim soldiers from India pray during the festival of Id al-Fitr in 1941.

Bren gun carrier

During a training exercise, troops of the 2nd Monmouthshire Regiment leap from a tracked vehicle called a Bren gun carrier that carried men and equipment.

Phoney war

For the first few months, there was no full-scale fighting on land. People called it the 'phoney war'. In Britain, soldiers trained, staffed coastal defences and manned anti-aircraft guns in case Germany invaded. In France, soldiers spent a hard winter, digging fortifications and living on army rations.

"... Us chaps who had been in the service were under no illusion as to what the word 'war' itself meant... I answered the call same as many thousands of others and reported myself at Winchester... literally hundreds and hundreds were pouring through the gates... all reserves answering the call...**"**

Edward Doe, reserve soldier

Women auxiliaries

More than 200,000 women served in the army during the war. They worked as cooks and despatch riders, and operated anti-aircraft guns.

The women's branch of the army was called the Auxiliary Territorial Service (ATS). It was formed in 1938. At first women volunteered. From 1941, they were conscripted, like men.

Early start

At first the ATS was not as popular as the Women's Royal Naval Service (WRNS) or Women's Auxiliary Air Force (WAAF). Early recruits often did not get their full khaki uniform and some had to drill in civilian clothes. Most people thought women could not do the same work as men so at first women were used as cooks and clerks.

More duties

As more men were needed to fight, more women joined the ATS and their work expanded. The ATS were drivers, mechanics and engineers. They operated teleprinters, receiving and sending messages, sometimes in code. Women could be sent anywhere in Britain. Three hundred went to France in 1939.

Drivers

An ATS despatch rider on her motorcycle. ATS women drove every kind of vehicle from ambulances to staff cars and heavy lorries. They also repaired and maintained the vehicles.

Plane spotters

Two ATS 'spotters', one with binoculars, search the skies for incoming enemy aircraft. Many anti-aircraft gun sites were in bleak inhospitable areas. It was very cold watching for aircraft at night.

Targeting aircraft

People did not think it was right for women to fire guns and kill people. But many ATS worked on anti-aircraft batteries. They operated predictors and range finders, pinpointing enemy aircraft so they could be shot down.

Marching and drill

Women marched, drilled and went on route marches the same as male recruits. They lived in barracks or Nissen huts, in basic conditions. Often toilets were wooden huts over pits. Army discipline was strict. But women gained independence and were proud of being able to serve.

Mechanics, 1942

ATS women move a gun turret into position on a tank. Many women worked as electrical and mechanical engineers. They worked 12 hours a day, 6 days a week.

Recruits

Officers were often privileged women. Other recruits had been hairdressers, typists, teachers or shop workers. From 1943 the ATS recruited from Commonwealth countries. Jamaica's first ATS Unit was formed in 1944.

Retreat

The phoney war ended in April 1940. German forces swept through northwest Europe. British and French soldiers were forced to retreat.

British soldiers had spent a bitter winter in France training and building fortifications. With reinforcements, the British Expeditionary Force (BEF) now numbered more than 390,000 men but they were still under equipped.

Retreating

British soldiers march towards Dunkirk, withdrawing from France. It was hot and sweat poured off the soldiers as they trudged along carrying guns and ammunition.

Lightning attack

Between April and May, Germany launched a *Blitzkrieg* or lightning war. They invaded Denmark and Norway, occupied the Netherlands, Luxembourg and Belgium and advanced on France. Allied forces fought but were no match for Germany's fast moving Panzer (tank) Divisions and well-armed infantry.

❝We got into Dunkirk around five o'clock in the evening — we hadn't eaten and it was really chaos. The sand was littered with bodies and... chaps all hoping to get off.❞

Leonard Howard, 201 Field Company, Royal Engineers, retreating to Dunkirk

Exhaustion

Soldiers arrived at Dover exhausted and dressed in whatever clothes they had (see next page). Trains were waiting to take them to London.

Retreat

The BEF fought a rearguard action from Belgium back to Dunkirk. They came under constant fire and engaged with German forces on the way. Some were captured and taken prisoner. Many were killed or wounded. Units became separated and streams of refugees hampered their retreat.

Evacuation

Footsore and hungry, the BEF arrived at Dunkirk. Some marched in formation; others straggled in. Soon the beaches were packed with thousands of wounded, exhausted men. As soldiers hunkered down, the Luftwaffe bombed the beaches. There was no cover.

In Britain, the Royal Navy organised an evacuation. Hundreds of warships and civilian craft crossed the Channel to rescue the BEF. It was an amazing operation. By 3 June more than 338,000 soldiers had been evacuated. Their heavy weapons had been abandoned but the bulk of the BEF had been saved.

> **"** ... Wheeler... was hit in the stomach by a machine gun... a further burst of fire took the top of his head off... At 21 years old, one hadn't experienced death and people being killed...**"**
>
> *Leonard Howard, 201 Field Company, Royal Engineers*

Evacuation, 1940

Standing in orderly lines, British soldiers wade out to a waiting destroyer moored off Dunkirk. One British soldier said they looked like London bus queues.

Desert war

For three years British and Commonwealth soldiers fought German and Italian forces in the deserts of North Africa. Conditions were unlike anything most soldiers had ever experienced.

In 1940 Italy joined the war on Germany's side and invaded Egypt from Libya but the smaller British army overwhelmed them, taking thousands of prisoners. Germany sent its famed Afrika Korps to assist Italy, and laid siege to Tobruk. For months the two sides chased each other over the desert. Finally, in 1942, Britain's Eighth Army defeated German forces in two battles at El Alamein. It was the first major Allied victory of the war. Soon after, Axis forces were driven out of North Africa.

Dust and smoke, 1942

British infantry charge forward through clouds of sand and dust during the Battle of El Alamein. The battle lasted for 12 days from 23 October to 4 November 1942.

Hostile landscape

The desert was a hostile environment. During the day the sun blazed down and at night it was freezing cold. Tanks and infantry churned up sand, making visibility impossible. Water and food were scarce and sandstorms could trap men in their tanks for days. Soldiers became ill

"… We had to put up with the extremes of heat and cold — the sandstorms… the flies… the shortage of water, the monotony of daily… bully beef and biscuits — and the fear…"

Fred Rosier, Squadron Leader, 229 Squadron, RAF

> **"**Our... lads had... to start making a gap through a British minefield. They went out without many mine-detectors, digging their bayonets into the ground... As soon as they found a mine, they'd tie a wire to it, then... yank the mine out...**"**
>
> *John Longstaff, Sergeant, 2nd Battalion, Rifle Brigade*

with dysentery, or ulcers and fever caused by sand flies. They dug into the sand, picked their way through minefields and fought with guns, shells and tanks.

Eighth Army

The British Eighth Army was formed in 1941 and became one of the best-known units of the war. It included Canadians, New Zealanders, Australians, South Africans and soldiers from Nazi-occupied Europe. One division — the 7th Armoured Division — was nicknamed 'The Desert Rats'.

Deadly mines

A mine explodes close to a British truck, which is carrying infantry. Both sides laid mines in the desert. Tanks and infantry had to negotiate around them, and there were many casualties.

Christmas dinner, 1942

An anti-aircraft crew celebrates Christmas in the desert. Christmas dinner is bully beef decorated with camel thorn, a spiky desert shrub.

The war in Italy

Between July 1943 and June 1944 Allied forces fought a campaign in Italy, with some of the bitterest fighting of the war. Casualties were very high on both sides.

Salerno, 1943

British soldiers fire a mortar at Salerno. British and American forces landed on 9 September and came under German attack. Fighting was intense. For a week, Allied forces were trapped, finally breaking through on 16 September.

Following victory in North Africa, Allied commanders planned an invasion of Italy. It began when Allied forces landed in Sicily in July 1943. Italy surrendered in September but the Allies met heavy German resistance on the mainland.

Slow advance

While some Allied troops moved from Sicily across the Messina Straits into southern Italy, another large force launched an assault at Salerno on the mainland. They were met with heavy German opposition and the advance northwards was very slow. Conditions were dreadful, particularly as a bitter winter set in. Fast-flowing rivers, hills and rocky terrain slowed progress. Soldiers were often bogged down in mud or snow.

"Just before Christmas we had taken a place called Casoli… the snow really came down. We were just below a ridge about ten feet high…I was found absolutely snowed under and had to be dug out…"

Gus Platts, 6th Parachute Battalion

Fierce fighting

Some of the heaviest fighting took place around Monte Cassino, the mountain, where Allies attacked entrenched German forces in December 1943 and were defeated. In January 1944 the Allies launched another assault at Anzio, higher up on the west coast of Italy. The landing surprised the Germans, but there were delays moving inland. German forces regrouped, leading to four months of fierce combat.

Liberating Rome

Four major battles were fought at Monte Cassino, with heavy casualties. Finally, in May 1944, Allied forces, backed by a major air offensive, broke through German defences. They liberated Rome on 4 June, two days before the D-Day landings in Normandy.

Ruins, 1944

Allied forces enter the ruins of Cassino. Fighting from an ancient monastery at Monte Cassino, German forces defended Cassino until British and Polish troops finally forced the Germans to retreat in May 1944.

Liberation, 1944

Nearly a year after the start of the Italian campaign, American troops enter Rome in June 1944. Cheering civilians welcome their arrival.

Caring for the wounded

Thousands of soldiers were wounded during the war. Doctors and nurses cared for the wounded on the battlefield, and in hospitals at home.

Medical personnel were either part of the army, subject to the same military rules and discipline as soldiers, or civilians. They could be posted anywhere. They worked in general hospitals and specialist burns units in Britain, and in field and emergency hospitals in Europe, North Africa and the Far East. More than 1,000 nurses treated the wounded at Dunkirk during the evacuation.

Front line surgery

Doctors perform emergency surgery on a wounded soldier. Field hospitals such as these often consisted of tents near the front line. They could be packed up and moved quickly if the enemy advanced.

On the front line

Doctors, nurses, stretcher bearers and ambulance personnel sometimes worked directly on the front line, rescuing and treating the wounded straight from the battlefield. It was a dedicated and dangerous occupation. They worked long hours, often under enemy fire, providing help in makeshift casualty stations until the wounded could be moved further back behind the lines. Medics dressed wounds in the open, and worked in makeshift field hospitals that could be tents or bombed out buildings.

❝… we had to deal with some terrible cases… we were bombed all the time… It was terribly hot and sometimes when the bombing was bad, we'd have to get patients under the bed… I remember one of the girls writing a letter for one man… after he'd been shot in the eyes…❞

Evelyn Cottrel, British nurse in North Africa

Dreadful wounds

Nursing staff and doctors saw dreadful wounds: soldiers with stomach, facial or head wounds, serious burns, and men who had lost limbs in explosions. In North Africa and Asia, medics also had to treat soldiers with tropical diseases such as dysentery or malaria. They treated Allied and enemy wounded, and civilians.

> **"**... all night long the wounded passed through... where I was medical officer. There was little we could do except stop any bleeding, give morphia (pain relief) and then evacuate them during lulls to the 80th Para Field Ambulance in a little dip about 200 yards away...**"**
>
> *Captain F G Nield, 153 Gurkha Parachute Battalion, Burma*

As the war neared its end, medical staff treated survivors of concentration camps and helped to care for refugees, uprooted by six years of war.

Nurses

A military nurse dresses a soldier's head wound in a hospital in France. About 9,000 British women served with the Queen Alexandra's Imperial Military Nursing Service during the war, treating wounded soldiers at home and abroad.

Feeding the troops

People often say an army marches on its stomach. Food was important for soldiers not just for energy but also because having a meal was comforting when soldiers were stuck in a war zone, far from home.

Soldiers often grumbled about food but the army did the best it could to feed soldiers well. Troops in training camps and barracks ate in the mess. Specially trained army cooks or the ATS prepared meals. Food in Britain was rationed, and army cooks used the same rations as civilians.

Brewing up, 1944
Gunners of the 78th Field Regiment in Italy take a break from fighting and brew up a much-needed cup of tea.

In the field

Military cooks travelled with the army when regiments were posted abroad. Supplies were usually taken up to the front line from central stores further back. Sometimes there was fresh fruit and meat but most provisions were tinned. Soups and stews were cooked in mobile kitchens.

> **"**… there was a most appalling explosion…
> I thought it was a shell, but actually it was my
> supper, which had been on a primus stove,
> overheating and blowing up…**"**
>
> *Alexander Stanier, Commanding 1st Battalion, Welsh Guards, in France 1940*

Rations

When opportunities for cooking were uncertain, soldiers were given packs containing 24-hour rations. These consisted of enough dried and tinned foods for 24 hours, kept in a waxed box. Contents varied but included service biscuits (a hard type of bread), oatmeal, blocks of tea, bully beef, chocolate bars, chewing gum, tinned fruit, tinned jam, toilet paper, matches, sugar and powdered milk. In quiet periods, soldiers cooked up rations on primus stoves. There were also larger packs, containing enough rations for 14 men, jungle pack rations, and special 'brew up' kits, containing tea, sugar and powdered milk. Meals were not exciting but they were nutritious.

> **"... We had tinned stew, soya sausages, bully beef, and the diet wasn't much varied from that..."**
>
> Reuben Kitson, Sergeant, Royal Corps of Signals, in Burma 1942

NAAFI van

The NAAFI — Navy, Army and Air Force Institutes – travelled the war zones with mobile canteens. They provided cups of tea and sandwiches for Allied troops.

Christmas geese

Gunner Jack Ward holds up two geese that will provide his regiment with a Christmas dinner. Soldiers often raided farms in enemy or occupied territory looking for livestock, eggs or fresh vegetables to add to their rather boring rations.

Jungle warfare

From 1942 British and Commonwealth forces fought the Japanese in the Burmese jungles. Heat and disease made jungle warfare a dreadful experience.

In December 1941 the Japanese air force bombed the US Navy at Pearl Harbor, Hawaii. The USA joined the war on the Allied side and a new front opened in Southeast Asia. Japanese forces invaded the British colonies of Malaya (modern Malaysia and Singapore) and Burma (modern Myanmar), capturing thousands of British soldiers. British, Burmese and Indian troops were forced to withdraw some 1,600 kilometres to India.

Humidity, 1944

Carrying rifles and ammunition, British soldiers march through the Burmese jungle, where temperatures could reach 40°C humidity. Soldiers developed dysentery, malaria and other tropical diseases.

Deadly conditions

Burma was a harsh place to wage war. It had thick jungles, wide, leech-infested rivers, deep valleys and steep mountains. Roads hardly existed. Most British soldiers had no experience of jungle warfare: at night it was pitch black, and every sound was frightening. Marching through the

> **"**… At about two o'clock in the morning we were shot at. We all got down into the water… When we moved on, most of us had forty to fifty leeches hanging off us…**"**
>
> Lieutenant Michael Marshall, 4/5th Gurkha Rifles, in Arakhan state, Burma

jungle was exhausting. The Japanese were ruthless fighters who neither expected nor gave any mercy. Casualties were high and in the extreme humidity, wounds festered and became septic.

Recapturing Burma

It took the Allied forces three years to recapture Burma. Soldiers learned how to exist in the jungle. Special forces were created, such as the Chindits, guerrilla fighters who were dropped behind enemy lines. The army made more use of the RAF and US air force for supplies and bombardment. In 1944, after fierce hand-to-hand fighting, the Allies defeated the Japanese at Kohima and Imphal on the Indian-Burmese border, and launched an offensive into Burma, re-taking the country by May 1945.

Gurkhas

A Gurkha soldier carries a wounded comrade on his back. The Gurkhas, who were from Nepal, had served with the British Army since 1815. They used a curved knife called a kukri *and were fearsome fighters. One British soldier described them as 'lethal'.*

"We continued to fight by day and night. The position became utterly gruesome and macabre... littered with corpses which could not be buried... It was impossible to construct proper dug-down trenches, dysentery became rife..."

Captain 'Dicky' Richards, 50th Indian Parachute Brigade, Battle of Sangshak, 1944

Mules, 1944

An exhausted soldier rests after crossing the Chindwin River in Burma. Travelling through the jungle or up mountains, troops often used mules to carry supplies and equipment.

21

Tanks, bridges and sappers

Engineers played a vital role. They built bridges, roads and railways. They laid and cleared mines and kept the army moving. It was dangerous and daring work.

More than 280,000 men served as engineers in the British Army. Known as 'sappers', they were members of the Royal Engineers. They defended civilians on the home front, defusing bombs and creating defences, and served with the army abroad.

On the move

Keeping the army on the move was a mammoth task. Troops, tanks, supplies and equipment had to make their way through regions such as deserts and jungles where there were no roads. Sappers laid down tracks and roads for tanks and men, built bridges over rivers, and carved steps into mountainsides.

Demolition and deception

Sappers used their engineering skills to slow down enemy forces. They detonated and demolished bridges, railways and airfields.

Bailey bridge, 1944

Sappers build a bridge over a canal in Belgium so that Allied forces can advance. It is a Bailey bridge, first used by the military in 1942. It was made of pre-fabricated pieces, driven in on lorries and then locked together where needed.

Mine clearing

A Royal Engineer carefully lifts a mine in Tunisia that has been laid by enemy forces. Sappers used special flail tanks to sweep minefields, or worked by hand, probing the ground with a bayonet to find the mines.

They laid mines and booby traps to catch enemy forces unawares. They were masters of camouflage: in the empty spaces of the North African deserts, they built dummy tanks as decoys to fool the enemy.

Clearing the way

When Allied forces advanced for an assault, sappers went ahead to clear the way. Some sappers accompanied commandos on raids, blowing up harbours, port defences and oil refineries. Sappers cleared paths through minefields, by hand or with special flail tanks that used a rotating cylinder of chains that whirled around, exploding mines infront of them.

Funnies

Sappers used specially adapted tanks for all sorts of difficult jobs. They called them 'funnies'. This odd-looking tank was a 'carpet-layer'. It was used to lay tracks on soft sand. Others had ramps that could be used as bridges, or bulldozer attachments. Some could even float.

"My party… were going to do the dry dock demolitions. Our team was responsible for the demolitions in the pumping stations, another for the winding stations… another for blowing the gate… other demolition parties [had] the job of destroying all the other dock machinery…**"**

Captain Robert Montgomery, Royal Engineers, attached to No 2 Commando, attack on St Nazaire, 1942

Entertaining the troops

Comedians, actors and musicians entertained troops throughout the war. They performed at home and in all the theatres of war, often under very difficult circumstances.

The British organisation that entertained the service personnel was known as ENSA, which stood for Entertainments National Service Association. It was sometimes nicknamed 'Every Night Something Awful' because some of the shows were not very good. But they were popular and they boosted morale. Troops greeted them enthusiastically.

Greeting the troops

ENSA 'glamour girls' greet troops in North Africa. For soldiers stuck out in the desert, a long way from home and girlfriends, these young women brought fun and memories of home.

Artists

ENSA started in 1939 as part of NAAFI which stood for Navy, Army and Air Force Institutes. The first concert was held at Old Dene Camp in Surrey; its last show was in India in 1946. Well-known stars of the day such as singer Vera Lynn, comedian Tommy Trinder, performer George Formby, and actress Vivien Leigh, joined ENSA to help the war effort. So too did lesser-known performers, some of whom became stars after the war.

Castle steps, 1944

Standing on the steps of a French chateau, ENSA puts on a concert for British troops in France. Performances varied from sentimental popular songs of the day through to classical concerts.

War zones

ENSA put on shows and sketches wherever troops were based. They travelled in all sorts of vehicles from tanks to rickshaws, taking their own generators, musical instruments and even mobile stages. They lived in basic accommodation and went directly into war zones. ENSA entertained troops in Europe and North Africa and put on shows in India and Burma. They followed the troops over the English Channel and into France in 1944, when the Allies invaded Normandy. By the end of the war, ENSA had given millions of performances.

Ukulele player, 1944

George Formby plays his ukulele for a small group of appreciative soldiers. Wearing helmet and battledress, Formby was the first to entertain British troops after D-Day.

> **"**After we left the Irrawaddy… we said, "…we want to go forward where there's no entertainment at all."… We had two jeeps. I sat in the front jeep, two soldiers, rifles at the ready. Dougie sat in the back jeep with the piano, which kept falling off…**"**
>
> *Nan Kenway, ENSA, performed with husband, Douglas Young*

The show must go on, 1943

Geraldo and his Orchestra, with singer Dorothy Carless, entertain airmen from a makeshift stage supported by oil drums at an airfield in North Africa.

Invasion and liberation

By 1943, the tide of war was turning in favour of the Allies. British and Allied troops prepared to invade France.

On 6 June 1944 after months of training and preparation, Allied soldiers were ferried across the English Channel and stormed onto the beaches of Normandy. More than 155,000 British, Canadian and American troops took part. They included commandos, infantry, artillery, engineers and tank troops. About 2,500 died during the invasion, many drowning or being mown down by machine guns. But the invasion was successful. By the end of June, some 850,000 men and 150,000 vehicles had been landed.

> **❝**All along the beach, there were men lying dead and not just in the waves. Some of them still had their tin hats on.**❞**
>
> *James Bellows, Signal Sergeant, 1st Battalion, Hampshire Regiment on landing at Normandy, 6 June 1944*

Onto the beaches

Sappers and infantry scramble onto the beaches at Normandy, France, under mortar and shell fire. In the background, medical orderlies help the wounded. Photographers recorded all aspects of the war, often risking their own lives.

Liberation

Civilians in occupied countries greeted British soldiers as liberators. Here British soldiers hand out chocolate to Dutch civilians, thousands of whom starved during the winter of 1944-45.

Liberating Europe

Allied soldiers soon found that moving further inland was no 'walk over'. There was bitter fighting around Caen, in France, and at Arnhem in the Netherlands. But, although the advance was slower than expected, by the end of the year, Allied troops had liberated France, Belgium and the Netherlands.

A shocking discovery

In December 1944 German forces made a final counter-attack in the Ardennes Forest, Belgium. They were defeated with huge losses and by February 1945 Allied forces were advancing into Germany. As British soldiers moved through Germany, they made a shocking discovery: a concentration camp at Bergen-Belsen, near Hanover. It was full of dead and dying prisoners, most of them Jews. British soldiers, who liberated the camp, were horrified. By the end of the war hundreds of camps had been discovered by Allied troops all over Germany.

Horror, 1945

British soldiers liberated Bergen-Belsen camp in April 1945. Sergeant Brewster of the Royal Artillery said survivors had, "terrible sunken eyes and they put their hands out to try and touch us. It was a complete shock… We didn't have the faintest idea."

Coming home

The Second World War ended in 1945, and soldiers began to return home. For many the transition to civilian life was difficult.

Germany surrenders, 1945

Soldiers eagerly grab a special edition of the independent American military newspaper Stars and Stripes, *which was published by the London* Times *on 7 May 1945. It announced that Germany had surrendered.*

American and British soldiers crossed the River Rhine, Germany, in March 1945. Adolf Hitler committed suicide in April, and on 8 May Germany surrendered. War in Europe ended but fighting continued in the Far East. Atomic bombs were dropped on the Japanese cities of Hiroshima and Nagasaki and Japan surrendered on 15 August. The Second World War was finally over.

Demobilisation

From June 1945 soldiers were stood down and shipped home. It was called demobilisation or 'demob'. It took months for all the soldiers to return. Some were badly wounded. Others had spent years in prison camps in Europe or Japan, and many were scarred by terrible experiences.

Demob

Carrying his kitbag, Rifleman John Neale, aged 31, of the King's Royal Rifle Corps, finally leaves his unit in Belgium to return home. He was the four millionth soldier to be demobilised.

Adjusting to peace

Most soldiers were delighted that war was over but many found it hard to adjust to peacetime. They had lost friends in the war and for many it was hard to forget the terrible scenes they had witnessed. Bombing had devastated cities and towns. Rationing was still in force and shortages got worse. It took time for soldiers to re-adjust to family life where children had not seen them for a long time, and wives had run the families in their absence. But slowly soldiers found jobs and settled back.

Building new lives

Before the war Britain had suffered economic depression. Servicemen and women, who had lost six years of their lives to war, wanted a better future. Following the war a newly elected Labour government introduced a welfare state and new building programmes. Conditions gradually improved.

> **"**After the war there were times when I was so depressed that I came close to suicide... wasn't so much that I was fed up with having survived the war or that... my friends had been killed... it was the future... I'd had six years taken away from me...**"**
>
> Corrie Halliday, 11th Hussars

Losses

Private Philip Johnson of the 2/6th Queen's Regiment gazes at British graves at Anzio, Italy, where nearly 5,000 British and American soldiers and sailors died in 1944. Worldwide 55 million people died in the Second World War. Nearly 400,000 British military personnel and civilians were killed.

Glossary

Allies The military forces of Britain and its empire, France, the USA, USSR and other countries during the Second World War.

Artillery Soldiers who operate large-calibre guns.

ATS Auxiliary Territorial Service, the women's branch of the British army.

Axis powers The military forces of Nazi Germany, Italy, Japan and some Eastern European countries in the Second World War.

Bergen-Belsen One of many concentration camps built by the Nazis.

Blitzkrieg German for 'lightning war'. Military tactic based on speed and surprise, using tanks supported by aircraft and infantry.

Bully beef Canned meat.

Chindits Allied special force, led by General Orde Wingate, which fought behind enemy lines in Burma.

Civilians Ordinary members of the public. Not part of the military.

Commando A member of the army, specially trained to do particularly dangerous and daring raids.

Conscription Compulsory military service.

Dysentery Severe and potentially fatal diarrhoea.

First World War (1914-18) Also called the 'Great War' or World War I. Fought between the Entente, which included Britain, France, Italy, Russia and the USA, and the Central Powers, which included Germany, Austria-Hungary and Turkey.

Humidity The amount of moisture in the air.

Infantry Soldiers who are trained to fight on foot.

Luftwaffe The air force of Nazi Germany.

Malaria A potentially fatal tropical disease spread by mosquitoes.

Nazi Short for National Socialist — an extreme right-wing political party led by Adolf Hitler. It controlled Germany from 1933-45.

Nissen hut A building made out of corrugated iron with a concrete floor. It was shaped like a tunnel.

Occupied countries The countries, including France, Poland, Belgium and the Netherlands, which were invaded and occupied by Nazi Germany.

Phoney war The period between September 1939 to April 1940, when there was little fighting on land.

Regiments Military units usually consisting of two or three battalions.

Second World War (1939-45) Also known as World War II. Fought between the Axis Powers, which included Germany, Italy and Japan, and the Allies, which included Britain and its Empire, France, Russia and the USA.

WAAF Women's Auxiliary Air Force, the women's branch of the RAF.

Welfare state A system of government that provides citizens with lifetime free health care and unemployment benefit.

WRNS Women's Royal Naval Service, the women's branch of the Royal Navy.

Further information
Books

My Second World War, Daniel James, Franklin Watts in association with the Imperial War Museum, 2008

Posters and Propaganda in Wartime, Daniel James and Ruth Thomson, Franklin Watts in association with the Imperial War Museum, 2007

Growing Up in World War Two, Catherine Burch, Franklin Watts, 2009

The Second World War, Dennis Hamley, Franklin Watts, 2007

Some useful websites

http://www.iwm.org.uk/
Website of the Imperial War Museum, which contains lots of information about the Second World War.

http://www.bbc.co.uk/ww2peopleswar/
BBC website which has lots of stories and recollections from people who served during the Second World War.

http://www.national-army-museum.ac.uk/
Website of the National Army Museum, which includes information on black and Commonwealth soldiers.

http://caber.open.ac.uk/schools/stanway/index.html
Website with information about women at war. Includes information on the ATS.

Note to parents and teachers:
Every effort has been made by the Publishers to ensure that the websites in this book are suitable for children, that they are of the highest educational value, and that they contain no inappropriate or offensive material. However, because of the nature of the Internet, it is impossible to guarantee that the contents of these sites will not be altered. We strongly advise that Internet access is supervised by a responsible adult.

Index